How to Help Your Child Achieve Academic Success in School

Educating Your Child During The Elementary, Middle, and High School Years

Christopher Harrison, M.ED.
NNeka Harrison, M.ED.

How to Help Your Child Achieve Academic Success in School

Christopher Harrison, M.ED.
NNeka Harrison, M.ED.

Published by

Inward Journeys Consulting
PO Box 18964
Oakland, CA 94619
Office/Fax: 1-866-285-6259
E-mail: inwardjourneysconsulting@myibocs.com
Home Page: www.inwardjc.net

Printed in the USA

All Praises To God, Special Thanks To Our Friends, Family, Antoine Frazier, And Mwalimu Baruti For Supporting And Encouraging Us On Our Journey

Dedication

To our children Ngozi and Aziza
and
To our parents
Rosalyn, Shelia and Norman

About the Authors

Born and raised in Oakland, California, Christopher and NNeka Harrison is a husband and wife team committed to education and family values. Together, they share over 10 years of experience in the following areas: facilitation/ mediation, academic/life skills instruction, curriculum development, research and evaluation, motivational speaking and program planning. Christopher has a B.A. in Urban Planning from Morehouse College and an M.ED. with an emphasis in Teaching from Mills College. NNeka has a B.A. in Criminal Justice from Clark-Atlanta University and an M.ED. in Educational Leadership with an emphasis in Early Childhood Education from Mills College. Their passion for education has led them to pursue published works in the interest of children and families.

Table of Contents

A Note from the Authors

Before we begin with our discussion about your child's educational future, we would like to congratulate you on making a decision to read the contents in this book. You see, we believe it takes a certain kind of parent or guardian to even begin to consider the ideas, opinions, and comments of another person—especially when it concerns the well-being and future of his/her child. Lets be honest, there are definitely some parents or guardians out there who are simply not willing to accept any advice from anyone when it comes to rearing and raising their child for academic and lifelong success. So, if you are reading this book because you want to begin the process of enhancing your framework for parenting your child in school, then you deserve a medal for your humility, resourcefulness, and your commitment to your child's future.

Now that you have begun one of the preliminary steps toward helping your child develop the habits he/she needs to enhance his/her academic performance, we would like to request that you allow us to address all of you who may read this book as *parents*. It doesn't matter if you are a grandparent, aunt/uncle, distant cousin, coach, mentor, or biological mother/father. If you have any degree of influence in a child's decisions, then you have the privilege, pleasure, and opportunity to rear and raise that child towards educational greatness. Hence, we call each of you who are reading this book *parents*, because a parent is simply someone who fosters in a child the capacity to lead a successful life while ensuring that he/she obtains the best education possible.

Are you wondering what motivated us to write this book? Well, that's easy. For starters, we are currently parents of two toddler-aged children and this has compelled us to develop our perspective on educating/parenting our own children for a successful future. Also, in light of the current climate of national and statewide budget cuts in education, we believe parents should prepare themselves (and their children for that matter) to take on even more of a responsibility of helping their children achieve academic success. We, too hear of the dismantling of after-school programs, teacher lay-offs, and the warnings of classrooms busting from their seams with more students than a class can accommodate. We are also aware of the current debate about who is responsible for the alarming rate of student failure, low academic performance, and the development of attitudes/behaviors that contribute to low self-esteem and juvenile delinquency.

So when we took into consideration our current disposition as parents along with our awareness of the plight of education for struggling students, distressed parents, and poverty-stricken communities, we became compelled to make an attempt to strengthen and rebuild our families and communities by focusing on the education of our children, at-large. *We believe parents are the primary educators of their children.* With this in mind, we seek to partner with parents to help them maximize their influence as positive and aggressive socializing agents for their own childrens' future.

There is power in ideas. Simply put, ideas are the engine of any society. If we, as parents, want our children to succeed academically and in life, we are going to have to build our mental frameworks for educating our children. This means we must develop the best possible understanding of the educational process in terms of how parents, students, and schools can work together to accomplish that lofty but attainable goal—academic excellence for all of our children.

With God as our guide along with our concerted efforts towards posterity (or preservation of our children's future), we can succeed in reversing the undesirable academic and social conditions of our children and help them to develop more constructive educational (and ultimately social) habits for lifelong success, peace, and productivity. Our primary source of motivation for writing this book (which is the first of many books to come) is summed up in the following biblical scriptures: "...and they said, Let us rise up and build...The God of heaven, he will prosper us; therefore we his servants will arise and build..." Nehemiah 2: 18, 20

Introduction

This book includes 9 conversational passages that have been written to help you build your capacity for rearing your child for academic and lifelong success. While reading, you may feel as if you are having a conversation with either a teacher, counselor, academic tutor, school administrator, youth and family specialist, or all of the above. If you find yourself having this kind of experience —then good! This is intentional!

We wrote this book for the purpose of allowing you to enter into several conversations with us concerning the academic habits and performance of your child. You will find this book deepening your understanding of the process of education from an educator's perspective. To help you build a framework to assert your right and power as primary educators of your own children, we have taken the liberty to expose you to our understanding of the process of education (based on our own personal experiences as each of the educational stakeholders mentioned in the previous paragraph).

After reading this book, we pray that you will become empowered to help your child develop a framework (or decision-making system), which will enable him/her to implement those habits at school that will lead to academic and lifelong success. Read, reflect, and rebuild...

Did Your Child Go To School Today?

Why is it important for your child to have consistent class attendance? How can poor class attendance affect your child's performance in school? What kinds of benefits are in store for your child if he/she has good, consistent class attendance?

It is no secret that your child needs to be in class on a daily basis. However, many of our inner-city school districts are plagued with poor, inconsistent class attendance. If you walk through the halls of some of our elementary, middle, and high schools, you will be surprised to see so many students roaming the halls during class time. Even a drive around the block within close proximity to certain schools will allow you to witness students cutting class while playing the dozens (clowning around), shooting craps, indulging in drugs, and/or other things that I will not mention.

The fact of the matter is, while you are at work your child may be on his/her way down a path of inconsistency (poor class attendance) that could lead to a limited education and a damaged future. If this sounds familiar, then it is imperative that you take the necessary steps to guard your child from the social and educational consequences of poor class attendance!

Your child should be in class learning from his/her teachers and peers as much as possible. The more your child learns, the brighter his/her future will become. When your child is in class consistently, your child will be able to keep up with daily assignments, hear about extracurricular opportunities, and get help from the teacher or his/her peers when needed.

You must remember that all teachers do not have the same grading scale and some teachers allow good class attendance to positively influence their grading. The student who has earned a 'B+' in Algebra may very well receive an 'A' on an account of his/her steady attendance record.

If your child develops a reputation of having an inconsistent, random attendance record, then you and your child may be in store for a roller coaster ride with counseling and therapy professionals, school administrators, and even the juvenile justice system. Your child's presence in class (on a daily basis) can shield you both from having to incur any headaches, frustrations, and stresses that may come from having to address issues of truancy in school.

A child who is not in class runs the risk of falling behind in his/her daily class and homework assignments. Not to mention the affect that missing test and quiz scores can have on your child's grading, it could possibly lower your child's academic grade by one or even two grade marks. If your son or daughter accumulates a bunch of zeros for missing assignments due to class absences, then the chances of earning higher grades will be reduced dramatically.

Oftentimes, a child who has missed a lot of class time returns to class almost clueless about what has been taught. This can have adverse affects on their motivation for learning, attitude towards the class, and even their behavior towards their peers. For instance, some students who have been out of class for long periods of time loose their drive for learning, especially when they discover that they have to make up a lot of work in order to catch up with the rest of the class. Other students with high-class absenteeism may find it difficult to work together with their peers when they feel so belittled by the obvious difference in what they know academically, and what their peers know (at least those students who have regular class attendance).

As a concerned parent, you do not want your child to experience any of the consequences of poor school attendance. You would rather they reap the benefits of consistent class presence such as: an increased understanding of the subject taught, developing confidence in their academic ability, availability of help from their peers and teachers, and an awareness of various kinds of educational options and opportunities that are often placed in the mailboxes of teachers. Remember, consistent and disciplined class attendance can enhance the quality of your child's educational experience.

We have considered the importance of class attendance, but we also need to focus on how your child should come to class everyday. In the next section, we will review the importance of your child coming to class prepared with learning materials.

Is Your Child Borrowing Class Materials Again?

Why should your child bring his/her own materials to class? How can your child's lack of preparedness for class affect his/her learning? What benefits are in store for your child when he/she comes to class ready to learn?

As a Math teacher, I have witnessed time and time again selected students stroll into my class unprepared to learn. Their lack of learning materials is usually most obvious because I often hear them asking their peers (and sometimes even me) for pens, pencils, paper, calculators, etc.

"Mr. Harrison, can I borrow a pencil. Mr. Harrison, I forgot my book again. Mr. Harrison, do you have an extra calculator." I must say that a student who comes to class without the basic materials to learn is not ready to learn at all.

I am telling you from experience that your child must come to class everyday with all of the materials that he/she needs to successfully participate in the classroom learning experience. When your child brings his/her tools for learning to class, your child makes a statement to the world that he/she is ready, willing, and able to engage in academic learning.

When your child brings his/her tools for learning to class, he/she can function as a student who is fully capable of learning without the hindrance of lack of resources—and we know this is one of the greatest social obstacles to success in any area of life including education.

I have observed how some unprepared students behave in my class. Some of them disrupt the lesson by constantly asking their peers for materials until they receive it. Others loose their focus and interest in the class lesson because they are tired of begging for what they need to participate in class. Yet there are even some students who come to class without the intent of learning anyway, and this explains why they did not make an attempt to bring their learning materials to class.

Whatever the case may be—I believe an unprepared child in a classroom is not ready to maximize his/her learning experience.

Lets consider the negative side effects of an unprepared child in a classroom. Without a pencil or pen, your child cannot produce work for the teacher to assess or evaluate for growth and learning. When your child comes to class without a textbook, your child may loose his/her drive to volunteer in class for anything because of the fear that comes along with drawing attention to his/her lack of preparedness.

If your child comes to class without a ready mind to learn, then all of the activities and teaching may have little affect (if any at all) on your child's learning. I have found this to be true in a lot of cases with certain students in class who are not ready to learn. As the saying goes, your child's mind is like a parachute—it cannot fly unless it is open. Therefore, a mind that is not ready to learn cannot fly because it is closed to any current that may pass through with the intent to take it to higher levels in education.

Just as I have observed the affects of a lack of preparation on a child's learning, I have also witnessed the positive affects of preparation on a child's educational development.

If your child comes to class with a mind ready to learn along with the basic and particular academic supplies (e.g. backpack, notebook, calculator, textbook, etc), then he/she will begin to take the initial steps toward a path that will lead them to academic success. Your child will be able to participate in class confidently. Your child will be able to produce schoolwork for teachers to review. This will allow teachers to provide your child with constructive feedback for further development.

If your child comes to class prepared to learn, then he/she will begin to develop habits that will open the doors of opportunity in education and in the various career fields of his/her choice.

Now that we have focused on the importance of your child coming to class prepared to learn, we will consider one effective way for your child to take charge of his/her education—by asking questions in class.

A Question Unasked Is A Question Unanswered!

Why do some students sit in class and never ask any questions? How can their lack of questioning in class affect their learning? Why should your child ask questions in class, especially when he/she is unclear about something that is being taught?

I know there are some students out there who do not ask questions in class because they are simply shy. However, I caution you to do some serious investigating with your child the next time he/she expresses fears about asking a teacher a question in class.

If your child is unmotivated, emotionally disturbed about unresolved personal issues, and/or preoccupied with the latest fads, clothing, and music artists, then asking questions in class may very well be the furthest thing from his/her mind. Simply put, it is very difficult for a child to be engaged in learning in class (by asking questions) when the daily lesson seems to be the most unimportant thing to them on their priority list.

Some students sit in class and refrain from asking questions because they are afraid that their peers may laugh at them. Other students keep their questions to themselves because they do not want to be seen as the nerd of the classroom. Whatever the case may be, while students go to school to learn, we often find that only a fraction of them aggressively take charge of their education by asking questions in class.

Raising questions in class is often considered to be a form of class participation. Some teachers even take this into account when grading students on their academic performance in class. This means that if your child does not raise any questions, then he/she may not receive the best grade possible.

I have found that the students who do not ask questions in class usually are the main ones who should be asking questions. There may just be a chance that what they think they know or understand is either inaccurate or a little underdeveloped. When testing time comes, underdeveloped or inaccurate information recorded on a test can result in lower test scores, tracking into less advanced classrooms, and/or routine visits to resource and educational specialists.

I believe every parent wants the best possible education for his/her child. Yet, we must remember that our children also have some responsibility in determining the quality of education that they receive. When your child either holds on to unasked questions, or refuses to seek new ground for his/her learning by way of questioning, then your child's learning will become limited to only what is initially understood. Or his/her learning may be stifled by a lack of understanding of the concepts, discussions, and activities that are delivered to them in class.

Unquestionably, these consequences can be avoided when students simply become more aggressive with their learning in the classroom. When your child begins to ask questions in class, his/her windows of learning will become opened to receive limitless information that will add excitement to the educational experience. Not only will your child increase and enhance his/her own learning, but peers will also benefit from the teachers' effort to bring more clarity to the concepts, discussions, and activities at hand based on the questions asked.

We must encourage our children to become co-constructors of their own knowledge by becoming active participators in their education. Challenge your child to seek learning beyond the teacher's daily lesson plan. Encourage your child to have inquisitive minds that not only consume information that is pre-developed, packaged and delivered from teachers, but also thirsty to consume information in response to their appetites for particular kinds of knowledge.

In other words, tell your child to glean from their teachers all the valuable knowledge they can receive. Remind them that a varied knowledge base will prove to aid them in the decisions that they are making now, as well as in the ones that await them in the future.

As we have considered how essential it is for your child to raise questions in class, we must also turn our attention to the importance of your child putting forth his/her best effort. It is the best effort of a child that can yield an optimized educational experience.

Is Your Child Just Getting By Or Putting Forth His/Her Best Effort?

Academic excellence is a topic that has been widely discussed in this country with respect to student performance in school. As a parent, this is a subject that you should not take lightly, because it is the effort of your child in school that can largely determine the kind of life that he/she leads upon completion of his/her secondary education.

Just what constitutes a child's best effort? How important is it for your child to put forth his/her best effort in school? What kind of relationship exists between a child's efforts in school and the habits that he/she is likely to continue to employ after high school?

I would like to define a child's best effort, academically speaking, as constituting the convergence of a child's wholehearted thoughts, actions, and resourcefulness in an attempt to achieve a desired educational goal. In other words, I believe a child puts forth his/her best effort in class when he/she consciously makes a decision to strive for excellence in all things academic.

In my experience as an educator, I have noticed how much of a disparity there is in the kind of effort that some students put forth while pursuing their education. Some students come to school with a mindset that they are going to do whatever it takes (within reason and with integrity) to achieve academic excellence in their classrooms. While other students either constantly come to class with a very lazy approach toward their learning or with the "do-enough-to-get-by" attitude.

Let me just say that your child's effort in the classroom is a very essential component of the educational experience. As the saying goes, you reap what you sow. If your child sows seeds of little effort into his/her education, then he/she will reap a harvest of very little learning. We must make it clear to our children that their educational experience in the classroom is like an input/output system. Whatever kind of effort they put into their learning will (to a significant degree) determine the quality of education that they receive in the classroom.

The primary and secondary years of education are a training ground for the kinds of life skills that your child will need to develop to function in this society. With this in mind, it is quite important that your child develop a habit of doing his/her very best in all things academic, social, and otherwise.

For instance, if your child develops a habit of rushing through his/her class and homework assignments, then he/she may carry this same habit into the job-world. This sense of anxiousness could very well result in careless mistakes costing a company a loss in revenue, business clients, or even the loss of his/her own job.

Everything that our children do in the classroom serves as a direct reflection of who they are internally. Hence, if a child's current identity is synonymous with a sluggard, then this characteristic is going to reveal itself in the quality of his/her work, attitude towards learning, and effort towards acquiring a quality education.

As adults, we all know how difficult it is to break habits that are not good for us. We are also familiar with how some of these bad habits have functioned as setbacks, stumbling blocks, and obstacles to our own personal growth and development. For the record, let me reiterate to you that if your child does not put forth his/her best effort in the classroom in terms of receiving and accepting academic assistance, completing assignments, and studying daily, then he/she may become guilty of setting limitations on the development of his/her own academic capabilities.

Simply put, your child really and truly holds the key to unlocking the doors of a promising educational experience in the palm of his/her own hands. Tell your child that he/she cannot continue to attend class and, figuratively speaking, crack his/her head open and expect teachers to pour all the knowledge in.

Your child must aggressively pursue his/her education with great zeal and a passion with the intent to acquire and develop a knowledge base that will prove to be beneficial in the social, political, and economic decisions that he/she will make in the later years to come. We will now turn our attention to discussing other specific habits in the classroom—such as the importance of note taking.

Class Notes?
Who Needs Them?

Information from the teacher, coupled with the documentation and processing of information by the child leads to learning. I believe this is true for all cases of students in the classroom.

Has your son ever allowed you to see his class notes for the day? Maybe you've heard your daughter exclaim, "I don't need to take notes in class because I already know this stuff!"

You would be surprised to hear how many different kinds of excuses students come up with to explain why they do not jot down notes in class. We will direct our attention to the following key points about your child's note-taking in class: 1) Class notes help your child remember key concepts 2) Class notes is an introduction to the importance of documentation for your child 3) Class notes help your child become responsible for his/her own learning.

Let's reflect a moment to a time when you were a student during your teenage years. Did you ever get frustrated while working on a homework problem in math? Did a teacher ever call on you in class and ask you to bring your class notes to the board to explain a concept or a key theme? Did you ever fumble through several sheets of paper trying to find some information to help yourself prepare for a test or quiz? I wonder if you answered yes to any of these questions. I know I did, and let me just say that there is also a chance that your child may be able to answer yes to either some or all of these questions as well. We will now consider the importance of note-taking in class.

Class notes serve as an emergency cushion to help your child remember certain ideas, themes, concepts, and/or problems that may have been explained by the teacher. Consequently, if your child does not copy down notes from the teacher's board or jot down notes from the daily lectures, then there is a high possibility that your child may not remember key points or explanations from the daily lesson.

I once heard someone say "what gets written down gets completed". You and I know that one of the most important life skills that our children will ever need is the skill of documentation. When your child neglects to write down any assignment, sooner or later your child will find him/herself asking the teacher for another opportunity to turn in the assignment that he/she probably forgot to complete.

Also, it is essential that your child understand how important it is for him/her to develop a habit of writing down key information during class time. For example, if a teacher makes a mistake in his/her written notes on the board and your child ends up writing a wrong answer on a test because of this mistake, then your child can approach the teacher (with confidence and proof) to identify the error in his/her class notes. I believe any teacher with integrity would be willing to change the grade on your child's exam with this kind of evidence.

Needless to say, your child's learning does partially rest on the teacher's ability to transmit information effectively and clearly to students in the classroom. However, your child must also bear some of the responsibility for learning by making a conscious decision to take charge of his/her own education. One of the ways your child can take charge of his/her own learning is by writing down things in class to study and reflect on to cultivate a deeper understanding of the subject matter at hand.

Your son or daughter can also position him/herself to become one of the students who always has the class notes from any particular day's lesson to pass on to a peer who may have been absent from class. Hence, your child's preparedness (by way of note-taking in class) will begin to have a positive ripple effect on the learning of his/her peers in the classroom.

It is no secret that the act of documenting information has been around in this world we live in for a long, long time. Yet, whether or not our children are aware of the importance of documenting information is another question for us to consider. I would like to encourage you to help your child practice this skill of documentation through the act of note-taking in the classroom. Once your child develops a respect for taking notes in class, he/she will begin to experience the academic and social benefits of this most needed skill.

Writing down key concepts, assignments, etc. is a critical component of your child's learning experience in the classroom—so is completing and turning in all class-related assignments. We will discuss this academic habit in the next section.

Are You Aware That Your Child Might Be Missing ____ # Of Assignments?

As an educator, it has always been puzzling for me to understand why some of our students actually believe that they do not have to turn in all of their class assignments. Usually, those students who do not turn in their schoolwork on a consistent basis end up earning the poorest grades in their classes.

I would like to talk to you about several reasons why your child should always turn in all of his/her class-related assignments. I believe this kind of academic consistency can help enhance your child's overall grade in the classroom, as well as allow him/her to receive some helpful feedback from teachers. This will aid your child in moving closer toward realizing his/her academic potential in the classroom.

It is certain that a child who randomly turns in class assignments can expect to earn lower assessment scores and school grades, receive several parent phone calls home, and achieve a lower level of competency and understanding of what is taught in the classroom.

Lets consider the reasons why these projections are true. First of all, your child's academic grades rely partially on his/her performance on class-related assignments. All teachers need some way of evaluating and assessing your child's academic performance. Some of the most common types of generalized class-related assignments that are often factored into your child's grading are: class and homework, tests/quizzes, journals, portfolios, and projects. These tangible deliverables often require teachers to evaluate and assess them to determine evidence of growth and development, areas for improvement, and to identify indicators of additional need for academic assistance.

If your son or daughter neglects to turn in his/her assignments on a consistent basis, then he/she may earn a class grade that was produced from an average that included a bunch of "zero" entries in the teacher's gradebook. Simply put, the more "zero" entries that your child receives in a teacher's gradebook, the lower your child's grade will fall.

I have seen this happen far too often for certain students, and it usually occurs at the expense of their own learning. When your child neglects to turn in class-related assignments, then your child forfeits his/her opportunity to receive constructive feedback from a teacher. Your child will miss out on an opportunity to receive the kind of feedback that will help enhance his/her understanding of the subject matter under study.

It is quite difficult for teachers to identify indicators of an academic need when there is no work to assess or evaluate. For instance, modified curricula, tutorial assistance, and/or culturally relevant teaching techniques can be proscribed for certain students who require a diversified kind of learning experience in the classroom. However, when your child does not provide his/her teacher with any work to review and reflect on, certain indicators of an academic need may go undiagnosed for long periods of time. Undiagnosed learning styles, disabilities or differences, and academic deficiencies can further complicate your child's educational experience in the classroom so please—do not take this lightly!

As a concerned and dedicated parent, you have to help your child understand the importance of turning in class assignments on a consistent basis. Remind your child that his/her course grades, academic performance, as well as his/her understanding of concepts in the classroom can be negatively affected by missing class-related assignments.

Also, if you do not want to spend a lot of time meeting with teachers about your child's missing class assignments, then I suggest that you see to it that your son or daughter is completing and turning in all of his/her schoolwork.

Lastly, we must always encourage our children to turn in quality work. Tell them that the quality of their schoolwork is a direct reflection of their commitment to learning, the amount of time they spend on completing the assignments, and their attitude towards their own education.

In the next section, we will devote our attention to a form of academic decorum that often is difficult for our children to grasp a full understanding of—that is, academic conversation in the classroom.

What Kind Of Conversation Is Your Child Having In Class?

Are you aware of the kind of conversations that your child may be having in class? Does your child know what is the difference between academic conversation and casual conversation? Is your child clear about the value of academic conversation and how it can enhance his/her own educational experience in the classroom?

Some teachers find themselves making endless phone calls home to speak with parents about their child's conversation in the classroom. Some students enter the classroom using such vulgar language, that it serves as a thorn to the ears of those it falls on. Other students interrupt their peers during class discussions without regard or respect for their classmates. Then there are those students who choose to have sidebar conversations with their partners at the wrong time during class time.

Do you know what kind of conversation your child is having during class time? Some parents find out about their child's conversational habits from mandatory meetings with teachers. Other parents tend to find out about their child's classroom conversations by having tireless phone conversations with teachers. Yet, there is still something else that you can do to stay abreast of your child's conduct in the classroom. Yes, you guessed it—random classroom drop-ins are classic and appropriate.

As a parent, you can randomly check on your child's classroom conversation by sitting in on some of his/her classes. This will give you some first hand knowledge of how your child's academic conversation is developing or digressing.

As soon as you finish reading this section, have a talk with your son or daughter about the difference between academic and casual conversation. Help them to understand that academic conversation includes discourse around all things that pertain to the teaching and learning of the subject at hand in the class. Remind them that casual conversation is the very opposite—it pertains to all things that are not related to the subject matter taught and learned in the classroom.

Academic conversation includes the use of language, concepts/ideas, and vocabulary that is related to what the teacher is charged with the responsibility of helping your child understand. It is true that knowledge is power, but so is language usage. Tell your child that it is imperative that he/she develops a sense of comfort with using academic language in the classroom. Explain to them how academic conversation will prepare them to converse with people in the professional world. As you and I know, a job offer, a career path, or college entrance can often be determined by the quality of one's conversation during an interview.

The benefits of good academic conversation are not bound by the timeframe after the secondary years of your child's education. There are many in-class benefits that your child can experience when engaging in scholarly conversation during class time. For example, teachers often select class representatives to participate in oratorical and debate competitions. Other teachers allow their students to lead class discussions about certain topics of interest. Students also participate in rewarding their peers for their oratory skills by electing them to represent the student body on the their "Student Governing" committees.

As you can see, each of the previously mentioned benefits or rewards for engaging in good academic conversation can have long-lasting, positive effects on your child's educational journey. Nevertheless, I must also mention that poor or untimely conversation during class time can set your son or daughter up for a great deal of disappointment, cause him/her to be labeled as a "class disrupter", and/or even result in removal from the class or school altogether.

I want to remind you that your child (or someone else's child for that matter) cannot focus fully on what is being taught in class when he/she is either talking out of turn, using vulgar language, speaking disrespectfully to his peers or just talking about things that are unrelated to the subject at hand. This inappropriate kind of conversation during class time will simply interfere with your child's learning and cause him/her to fall behind academically.

In the next section, we will examine how peer relationships can be mutually beneficial in the classroom. That is, your child can help someone in class as well as get help from other classmates.

I Don't Need Any Help...
I Can Do This On My Own!

Independence is a positive quality for our children to have. Wouldn't you agree? "I mean if our children are ever going to be somebody, they are going to have to learn how to depend on themselves!"

I have heard this kind of comment from many parents, but I must venture to say that this is only half of the truth. The other half is that our children are not islands that are totally separated and disconnected from one another. No, they do not exist in this world or in the classroom alone, and neither do we ourselves for that matter.

So, why do we place burdens on our children requiring them to travel this journey through their education without either helping one another or receiving help from their peers in the classroom? Is such an independent journey through education the best way to prepare our children to enter into a society that thrives off of the interdependence of humanity?

As we grapple with this topic concerning the value of an interdependent pursuit of education by our children, we must visit the potential pitfalls of an extreme independent pursuit of education in the classroom. Simply put—how can your child's rejection of help from other peers do more harm than good?

I have had the opportunity to teach certain students who resist help from their peers and it has not been a pretty sight to see. Usually, students who refuse to receive help from their peers end up falling behind in certain areas academically. In some cases, these students are the high achievers in their classrooms. However, their haughtiness and pride often ends up preventing them from reaching their full potential, academically speaking, because of their resistance against receiving assistance from their peers.

These high achievers end up building a false perception of their learning that is bound to fail when faced with a learning experience in the classroom that they do not understand. Let me say that this false perception of their learning often rests on their belief that they learned it all on their own. Even if a child learns from a textbook without the teacher's explanation, the child's learning is still tied to the explanatory efforts of the textbook writer. Learning is a mutual and interdependent experience in all cases!

If a child continues to reject outside help from others, sooner or later this same child will be faced with a situation that will require the assistance of another peer. If external assistance is continually rejected, this child may end up becoming extremely frustrated with his/her learning, loose a sense of time management during study time, and become an obstacle to his/her own learning.

Lets consider the child who seems to be struggling quite often in the classroom with understanding how to complete assignments correctly. When a child refuses to receive help from a fellow classmate, the child may find him/herself falling further behind in completing class assignments. This can become very discouraging for a child who has not experienced any academic successes in the classroom. I urge you to explain to your children the negative effects of resisting help from their peers in the classroom. Tell them that this can cause them to fall behind in their assignments, become frustrated, earn lower grades, and even loose their zeal for learning in the classroom.

As a math teacher, I know how difficult it is for any teacher to offer individualized attention to all of the students in the classroom. To address this issue, most experienced teachers rely on cooperative learning in the classroom to help maximize the learning experience for all of their students. This opens up the door for students to help one another, as well as receive help from one another in the classroom.

With this in mind, I would like to suggest that you encourage your child to help others in the classroom. When your child explains concepts to others, this in turn helps reinforce these same concepts in your child's mind. One of the best ways for your child to achieve mastery of certain concepts is to explain them to others—and the best place to practice their explanations is in their own classrooms with their own classmates. This mutual approach towards learning in the classroom will prepare your child for the interdependent, interrelatedness of humanity beyond the walls of the classroom.

Life after high school and college is often on your child's mind. In the next section, we will discuss why it is important for your child to seek connections between what he/she learns and real-life experiences. These connections will help inspire your child to pursue his/her learning with a passion and a purpose.

What Does This Stuff Have To Do With Anything, Anyway?

Has your child ever told you that she doesn't need to take a certain class in school in order to do what she wants to do in life? Maybe your son has shared with you his disregard for science because he believes he will not need to use any of that stuff in the future. How about this, has your child ever explained to you how certain concepts, ideas, themes, or class assignments are related to any real-life experiences or occurrences?

In order for your child to develop any type of respect or regard for education, your child must begin to see the usefulness and relatedness of education to life experiences and occurrences. For instance, if your child cannot see the relatedness of certain academic subjects to his or her own goals, then your child may loose enthusiasm for learning. We must remember that we are competing everyday with other flashy and persuasive kinds of societal influences that are trying to pull our children's attention in a direction that is often anti-educational.

Let me say that anything that has the potential to bring the very best out of our children is worth learning. Anything that has the potential to help our children achieve their personal dreams and also lead them to make positive contributions to society is worth learning. I must also assert that anything that is likely to lead our children away from what I just stated is not worth learning.

So, how do you handle a child who has just expressed disregard for learning any of the basic core subjects in school? Exposure. Conversation. Debate. Example. Challenge.

These one-word sentences reveal a particular role that you can play in assisting your child's teacher as you help him/her understand the usefulness and relatedness of education to real life situations. You can expose your child to experiences that may help him/her understand the connectedness of his/her educational experience in school with the outside world. You can have short or lengthy conversations and debates about how certain historical events are related to the current events of today. You can share with your child some of your personal experiences and explain how they are related to what they are being taught in their respective subjects in school. Lastly, you can challenge them to think "outside of the box" and figure out how certain core academic skills are related to certain employment-related skills.

Whose responsibility is it to identify potential connections between the subjects our children learn and the real-life experiences of the world we live in? Some educators believe it is up to teachers to explain connections between what they teach and real-life applications. Other educators believe it is the students' responsibility to perceive the relatedness between what they are learning in class and real-life experiences. I believe there is a shared responsibility between teachers, students, and parents that calls on each of them to help students bridge the gap between academic content and real-life situations.

With this in mind, here is where you—as a parent can come in. Challenge your son or daughter to try to find real life applications for what he/she is learning in their regular classes. As adults with more life experience we can point out and explain how certain academic ideas are tied to certain actual events, occurrences,

46

elements, experiences, and objects in life. For example, you can have a conversation with your child about the relatedness of his/her history review topics to the present-day events that are happening each day in this society we live in. Maybe you can take your child on a trip to the local bank to schedule meetings with bank tellers to ask questions about how important reading comprehension skills are to helping complete daily job duties.

Whatever the case may be, you must remember that parents are the first teachers and socializers of children. Since this is true, I believe parents have a natural edge and a special responsibility to help their own children see how intertwined their academic experiences are with the various fabrics of life.

Now, you may or may not understand all of the terms and concepts of every course your child is studying. However, you can challenge your son or daughter to seek connections between his/her classroom content and the events, people, and life experiences beyond the classroom walls.

Wrapping It Up!

Now that you have arrived at the end of this book, we would like to provide you with a table (See Appendix A) that will enable you to compare the habits of a *studious* and *non-studious* student. First, we encourage you to become familiar with these qualities, examine your child to see where he/she may fit, and then enter into a series of conversations with your child concerning the qualities indicated in the table.

We have provided two short surveys (See Appendices B & C) to help you focus your child's efforts toward becoming a *studious* student. Survey #1 is designed to allow parents to evaluate the quality of their own involvement in their child's educational experience. Survey #2 is designed to allow your child to evaluate his/her academic habits at school to identify areas for improvement. Suggestions have been included to provide you with a little direction as to where to begin concerning each area of improvement for both surveys.

If you find that you are in need of additional assistance with your child, do not panic—this is ok. Once you are able to comfortably and confidently identify your child's strengths and areas for improvement, we strongly suggest you contact local social service agencies, supplemental educational programs, and/or key educational stakeholders to partner with you in helping your child academically (See Appendix D). *Be patient with this process! You may find that some stakeholders and agencies are able to provide you and your child with direct academic services and others may simply be able to provide you with information and/or referral services.* We also encourage you to continue to develop your perspective on the process of education by reading other related texts, educational journals, and attending education-related conferences and workshops.

As you continue your journey of socializing your child to achieve educational and lifelong success, we encourage you to adorn yourself with patience, persistence, fortitude, resourcefulness, and optimism. And remember, you are simply cultivating your vineyard to yield fruit that will prove to be beneficial for your child, your family, your community, and humanity.

APPENDIX A

Comparative Habits of Studious / Non-Studious Students

STUDIOUS STUDENT HABITS	NON-STUDIOUS STUDENT HABITS
Consistent Class Attendance	Inconsistent Class Attendance
Brings Class Materials Daily	Borrows Class Materials Daily
Asks Questions When Unclear	Never Asks Questions In Class
Puts Forth Best Effort In Class	Does Just Enough To Get By
Jots Down Class Notes Daily	Rarely Takes Notes In Class
Completes All Class Assignments	Completes Some Class Assignments
Limits Talk to Academic Conversations In Class	Has A Lot Of Social Conversations In Class
Secures Help In Class When Needed	Never Seeks Help When Confused
Seeks Real Life Application of Learning Concepts	Unmotivated To Seek Understanding Beyond Daily Class Lessons

Note: After you have read this book, we encourage you to have a conversation with your child to find out what kind of study habits he/she currently possess. Next, meet with your child's teacher(s) to gain a clearer picture of his/her classroom study habits. After conducting this kind of evaluation of your child's study habits, you will develop a better understanding of some of the reasons for your child's academic struggles. Once you identify some of those *non-studious* qualities in your child, you can begin to start monitoring his/her academic habits to help keep him/her on track toward becoming a *studious student*.

APPENDIX B

Survey #1: Parent Self-Evaluation

This survey is designed to help you evaluate your own level of involvement in your child's education in terms of ensuring that he/she develops and maintains productive study habits for academic success.

<u>Directions:</u> Answer the questions below by simply circling "Yes" or "No".

1. Do you randomly check on your child's class attendance records?   Yes   No

2. Do you make sure that your child brings basic school materials to class daily?   Yes   No

3. Do you encourage your child to ask questions in class when he/she is confused?   Yes   No

4. Do you consistently remind your child of the importance of doing his/her best in school?   Yes   No

5. Do you randomly ask to see your child's class notes for each subject?   Yes   No

6. Do you contact your child's teacher(s) to verify whether or not he/she is turning in schoolwork on a daily basis?   Yes   No

7. Do you visit your child's class without notice to observe his/her classroom conversations?   Yes   No

8. Do you ensure that your child receives tutorial assistance, academic advisement, or motivational pep talks when needed?   Yes   No

9. Do you ask your child how his/her class lessons relate to real life situations?   Yes   No

<u>**Note**</u>: If you answered "No" to any of these questions, then by default you have just identified areas for you to focus on to help your child improve his/her study habits and become *a studious student*. You can use these questions to help monitor your own level of involvement in your child's educational success.

APPENDIX C

Survey #2: Student Evaluation

This survey is designed to help your child evaluate his/her own academic study habits. Allow your child to complete this survey either with you or independently.

<u>Directions</u>: Answer the questions below by simply circling "Yes" or "No".

1.	Do you have excellent class attendance?	Yes	No
2.	Do you bring your school materials to class every day?	Yes	No
3.	Do you ask your teacher questions in class when you are unclear about something being taught?	Yes	No
4.	Do you put forth your best effort as a learner in class everyday?	Yes	No
5.	Do you write down class notes everyday?	Yes	No
6.	Do you turn in all of your assignments?	Yes	No
7.	Do you limit your talk in class to academic conversations?	Yes	No
8.	Do you seek help from your teacher, tutors, peers, or advisors when you need it?	Yes	No
9.	Do you make attempts to understand how what you are learning relates to real-life situations?	Yes	No

<u>Note</u>: If your child answered "No" to any of these questions, then encourage your child to immediately make a commitment to turn the "No" responses into "Yes" responses. Encourage your child to be patient with this process, and offer as much support as possible. You can also contact one of your local educational stakeholders or national agencies (See Appendix D) to help your child develop an academic plan to improve his/her study habits.

APPENDIX D

Educational Organizations, Stakeholders, and Texts

NATIONAL ORGANIZATIONS	TARGETED GROUP
Omega Boys Club PO Box 884463, San Francisco, CA 94188 1-800-SOLDIER www.street-soldiers.org	Adolescent Boys & Girls
Boys & Girls Clubs of America 1230 W. Peachtree, Atlanta, GA 30309 (404) 487-5700 www.bcba.org	Children /Adolescent Girls & Boys
TRIO Programs 1025 Vermont Ave., Washington, DC 20005 (202) 347-7430 www.trioprograms.org	Children /Adolescent Girls & Boys
Girls, Inc. 120 Wall Street, New York, NY 10005 1-800-374-4475 www.girlsinc.org	Children /Adolescent Girls
United Way of America 701 N. Fairfax St., Alexandria, VA 22314 (703) 836-7112 www.unitedway.org	Children /Adolescent Girls & Boys
YMCA of the USA 101 N. Wacker Drive, Chicago, IL 60606 (312) 977-0031 www.ymca.net	Children /Adolescent Girls & Boys

EDUCATIONAL STAKEHOLDERS	AREA OF FOCUS
Professional Tutor	Academic tutorial assistance, study habits, assessments
Academic/Guidance Counselor	Academic advisement, career guidance, college readiness, advocacy
Educational Therapist	Learning disability assistance, behavioral / learning plans, diagnosis / intervention
Educational Consultant	Educational workshops, academic advisement, college assistance, advocacy, assessment
Educational Program Coordinator	Academic advisement, program admissions
Social Service Case Manager	Service referral, advocacy, community resources

Note: When contacting the agencies in Appendix D, you may find it useful to reference the table above as a guide to help you decide who can best assist you in helping your child based on his/her area of expertise.

Suggested Books / Authors

Suggested Books	Authors
Achievement Matters: Getting Your Child the Best Education Possible	Hugh Price
Becoming a Master Student	Dave Ellis
The Confident Student	Carol C. Kanar
A Black Student's Guide to Goal Setting	Baruti Kafele
The Study Skills Handbook	Judith Dodge